RANSOM KHANYE

Black Privilege

Transcending Racism

Cover design by Ransom Khanye
All copyrights reserved.

No portion of this book may be reproduced in any form without written permission from the author.

ISBN: 9798874338442

FOREWORD

In the kaleidoscope of human experience, the narrative surrounding race has been both complex and multifaceted. As we embark on the journey through the pages of "Black Privilege: Transcending Racism," we find ourselves at the threshold of a narrative that challenges conventional paradigms, seeks to dismantle stereotypes, and ultimately beckons us towards a world where unity triumphs over division.

This book is not a map with fixed coordinates but a vessel navigating uncharted realms—a journey of discovery that takes us beyond the surface of color and into the intricate tapestry of individual stories. As the foreword, my role is to extend an invitation, to beckon readers into a realm where preconceived notions are left at the door, and an openness to the nuances of human experience becomes the guiding compass.

The title itself, "Black Privilege," may stir a paradoxical sentiment in some. It is not an assertion of superiority or a denial of the historical injustices faced by black individuals. Instead, it serves as an entry point into a conversation about privilege that transcends the material and delves into the intangible—moments of grace, understanding, and acceptance that challenge the traditional narratives surrounding race.

Within these pages, a symphony of voices emerges—personal narratives that span continents and epochs, each contributing to the overarching melody of our shared humanity. From the tribal landscapes of

Zimbabwe to the snowy expanses of Romania, the stories unveil the resilience of the human spirit and the profound connections that transcend cultural divides.

Stereotypes, those limiting narratives that often confine our understanding of others, are dismantled within these chapters. Each story becomes a brushstroke, painting a portrait of authenticity that challenges the assumptions we may carry. By rejecting stereotypes, the book invites readers to see beyond the surface, to delve into the depths of individual experiences that defy categorization.

The emphasis on understanding behavior within the context of culture becomes a guiding principle—a recognition that behaviors are shaped by a multitude of influences, with culture playing a pivotal role. By exploring the richness of cultural contexts, readers are invited to step into the shoes of individuals whose stories unravel the intricacies of identity beyond the constraints of race.

At its core, "Black Privilege: Transcending Racism" is a testament to the power of unity. It envisions a world where the shackles of historical prejudices are broken, and the shared humanity that unites us takes precedence over the artificial divisions that seek to tear us apart. It is not merely an aspiration but a call to action—an encouragement for readers to reflect on their own biases, challenge their perceptions, and contribute to the collective effort of building bridges where walls have stood.

As you embark on this literary voyage, let the stories within these pages be a guiding light—a constellation that illuminates the path toward greater understanding, empathy, and unity. The journey will unfold through personal reflections, historical insights, and cultural explorations, offering a nuanced perspective on privilege, resilience, and the enduring power of human connection.

In closing, consider this foreword not as an introduction to a book but as an introduction to a conversation—a dialogue that extends beyond these pages and into the diverse landscapes of our shared existence. May the exploration of "Black Privilege: Transcending Racism" be an enlightening journey—one that challenges, inspires, and ultimately fosters a deeper appreciation for the rich spectrum of humanity.

With anticipation and gratitude for the journey ahead,

Ransom Khanye

Contents

Introduction: Black Privilege - Transcending Racism

In the intricate dance of human interactions, the threads of race, color, and cultural diversity weave a tapestry that, at times, reveals the scars of historical injustices. "Black Privilege: Transcending Racism" emerges as an exploration, a narrative that seeks to navigate the complexities of racial narratives and unveil the untold stories that defy conventional stereotypes. More importantly, it stands as a testament to the human capacity for understanding, unity, and the transcendence of divisions that have plagued societies for far too long.

This book is not a manifesto of grievances or a polemic against the injustices of the past. Instead, it is an invitation—an invitation to engage in a dialogue that moves beyond the traditional narratives surrounding race. It is a call to transcend the limitations of preconceived notions and delve into the intricacies of the human experience. Through the lens of personal stories, historical reflections, and cultural explorations, we embark on a journey that seeks to foster empathy, dispel stereotypes, and promote unity.

The title itself, "Black Privilege," may seem paradoxical in a world where the narrative of privilege often takes on a different hue. It is not an assertion that black individuals are inherently privileged; rather, it challenges us to reconsider what privilege truly means. The privilege explored within these pages is not about material advantages but about the silver linings in a tapestry often woven with threads of adversity. It is an acknowledgment of the moments of grace, understanding, and acceptance that transcend the limitations imposed by racial biases.

Stereotypes, those narrow and confining narratives that society often imposes, serve as barriers to genuine understanding. By rejecting stereotypes, we open ourselves to the vast spectrum of human experiences. This book endeavors to dismantle the stereotypes that perpetuate division, offering a nuanced perspective that invites readers to see beyond the surface and recognize the shared humanity that unites us all.

Understanding behavior within the context of culture becomes a pivotal theme in our exploration. It is a call to recognize that behaviors are shaped by a myriad of factors, with culture being a significant influencer. By emphasizing the importance of cultural context, we invite readers to move beyond the simplistic categorization of individuals based on color. Culture becomes the lens through which behavior is interpreted—a lens that unveils the rich tapestry of traditions, customs, and histories that shape our identities.

To understand behavior is to appreciate the intricate dance of cultural nuances. It is an acknowledgment that individuals, regardless of their racial background, are shaped by the traditions and values inherent in their cultural milieu. By embracing cultural context, we move away from the reductionist view that attributes behaviors solely to race, recognizing the multiplicity of influences that contribute to the mosaic of human identity.

At its core, this book is driven by a singular intention—to promote unity. Unity that transcends the artificial divisions carved by historical prejudices. Unity that recognizes the shared aspirations, joys, and struggles that bind us together. By delving into the stories within these pages, readers are invited to partake in a vision of harmony—a vision where the color of one's skin becomes but a brushstroke in the larger canvas of our shared humanity.

Promoting unity is not a solitary endeavor; it is a collective commitment that necessitates open hearts, empathetic minds, and a willingness to challenge our own biases. Through the exploration of personal narratives, historical reflections, and cultural insights, we hope to inspire a collective journey toward a world where unity is not an aspiration but a lived reality.

As we embark on this journey through the pages of "Black Privilege: Transcending Racism," let this introduction serve as a compass—a guiding light that illuminates the path toward understanding, acceptance, and unity. The stories that follow are not just individual narratives but windows into a world where privilege is redefined, stereotypes are shattered, and the human spirit prevails against the backdrop of racial complexities.

In unity and understanding, the journey unfolds.

Chapter 1: Echoes of the Past

In a world brimming with diversity, it's a tragic irony that we often reduce individuals to a set of preconceived notions based on the color of their skin. Stereotypes are pervasive, and they come in many forms, from casual assumptions to deeply ingrained biases. But in the pages that follow, we're setting out to shatter these stereotypes, one story at a time.

Stereotypes are dangerous for several reasons. They oversimplify the rich tapestry of human existence, reducing it to crude caricatures. They perpetuate division and discrimination, hindering the progress of societies as a whole. They blind us to the potential and the beauty that can be found in every corner of this world.

It's essential to recognize that behaviour is deeply influenced by culture and environment, not intrinsic racial traits. Imagine for a moment that you grew up in a different part of the world, surrounded by different customs and traditions. Would you not adapt and behave differently to fit in with the culture of your environment? Does that make you any better or worse than someone from another place? Of course not.

Every person is a unique combination of experiences, upbringing, and aspirations. We should celebrate these differences and embrace the richness they bring to our lives. When we reject stereotypes and take the time to truly understand individuals, we discover a world filled with captivating stories, perspectives, and potential friendships.

Throughout this book, we'll delve into personal stories, historical events, and acts of kindness that challenge stereotypes and reveal the incredible diversity within humanity. From Zimbabwe's tribalism to the Rwandese genocide, from Irish slavery to cultural exchange, these stories will shed light on the complexities of race, privilege, and the human experience.

As we embark on this journey, remember that our goal is not to promote division or reinforce stereotypes. Instead, we seek to promote unity and harmony among all races. There will always be extreme individuals who perpetuate cruelty, but they do not define the majority. People have been cruel to each other within their own races throughout history, just as they have across racial lines.

In each chapter, we'll explore real-life stories that challenge conventional wisdom and inspire change. Together, we will dismantle stereotypes, acknowledge the past, and work toward a future where every person is judged by the content of their character, not the colour of their skin.

Join us as we uncover the stories that demonstrate that there is no black privilege or white privilege; there is only human privilege—the privilege of understanding, compassion, and unity.

Chapter 2: No Stereotypes

In a world brimming with diversity, it's a tragic irony that we often reduce individuals to a set of preconceived notions based on the colour of their skin. Stereotypes are pervasive, and they come in many forms, from casual assumptions to deeply ingrained biases. But in the pages that follow, we're setting out to shatter these stereotypes, one story at a time.

Stereotypes are dangerous for several reasons. They oversimplify the rich tapestry of human existence, reducing it to crude caricatures. They perpetuate division and discrimination, hindering the progress of societies as a whole. They blind us to the potential and the beauty that can be found in every corner of this world.

It's essential to recognize that behaviour is deeply influenced by culture and environment, not intrinsic racial traits. Imagine for a moment that you grew up in a different part of the world, surrounded by different customs and traditions. Would you not adapt and behave differently to fit in with the culture of your environment? Does that make you any better or worse than someone from another place? Of course not.

Every person is a unique combination of experiences, upbringing, and aspirations. We should celebrate these differences and embrace the richness they bring to our lives. When we reject stereotypes and take the time to truly understand individuals, we discover a world filled with captivating stories, perspectives, and potential friendships.

Throughout this book, we'll delve into personal stories, historical events, and acts of kindness that challenge stereotypes and reveal the incredible diversity within humanity. From Zimbabwe's tribalism to the Rwandese genocide, from Irish slavery to cultural exchange, these stories will shed light on the complexities of race, privilege, and the human experience.

As we embark on this journey, remember that our goal is not to promote division or reinforce stereotypes. Instead, we seek to promote unity and harmony among all races. There will always be extreme individuals who perpetuate cruelty, but they do not define the majority. People have been cruel to each other within their own races throughout history, just as they have across racial lines.

In each chapter, we'll explore real-life stories that challenge conventional wisdom and inspire change. Together, we will dismantle stereotypes, acknowledge the past, and work toward a future where every person is judged by the content of their character, not the colour of their skin.

Join us as we uncover the stories that demonstrate that there is no black privilege or white privilege; there is only human privilege—the privilege of understanding, compassion, and unity.

This chapter sets the tone for the book, emphasising the importance of rejecting stereotypes and understanding behaviour in the context of culture. It also introduces the overarching theme of promoting unity and harmony among all races. If you have any specific additions or modifications you'd like to make, please let me know, and we can continue refining the text.

Chapter 3: Acknowledging Some Horrid Racist Practices

In the journey to understanding the complexities of race, privilege, and humanity, we must delve into the darkest corners of history. This chapter takes us to Zimbabwe, a nation where friendships blossomed despite the shadows of tribalism, but also a place scarred by the harrowing events known as the Gukurahundi killings.

Growing up in Zimbabwe, a land where tribalism often seemed deeply entrenched, I was fortunate to discover a profound truth – that friendships could transcend even the most divisive of barriers. Some of my closest friends, if not the very best friends I have ever had, were Shona-speaking. Despite the prevailing social climate that sought to indoctrinate us into hating one another, we shared the most beautiful days of our lives in our childhood.

The term "Gukurahundi" refers to a period of state-sponsored violence and brutality in Zimbabwe that unfolded in the early 1980s. It was a time when the unity that the nation had initially celebrated following its independence in 1980 shattered into a gruesome reality. The victims of this tragedy were primarily Ndebele-speaking Zimbabweans.

Led by the North Korean-trained Fifth Brigade, the government's crackdown on perceived dissidents resulted in the deaths of thousands. Reports of mass killings, torture, and widespread human rights abuses emerged, painting a bleak picture of Zimbabwe's post-independence journey. The scars left by the Gukurahundi killings continue to haunt the nation, as survivors and families grapple with the trauma and loss.

Acknowledging such atrocities is not only a moral imperative but also a critical step toward healing and reconciliation. It's about confronting the darkest chapters of our history, ensuring that the suffering of victims is not forgotten, and that justice prevails. Confrontation is not about assigning blame but about fostering understanding and a commitment to building a better, more inclusive future.

In this chapter, we've touched upon the personal experiences and friendships that flourished in Zimbabwe, even amid the shadow of tribalism. We've also explored the Gukurahundi killings, a painful and haunting chapter in Zimbabwe's history. By acknowledging these events and their historical context, we honour the memory of those who suffered and take a vital step toward breaking the cycle of racism and prejudice.

In the chapters that follow, we will continue to confront history, examine lesser-known narratives, and uncover stories that challenge conventional wisdom. Together, we can build a world where unity and understanding prevail over hatred and division.

Chapter 4: Rwandese Genocide

The Rwandese genocide, a dark chapter in human history, serves as a chilling reminder of the consequences of unchecked tribalism. This chapter aims to delve into the deeply personal stories of survivors, offering a narrative that transcends statistics and headlines, seeking understanding, empathy, and a call to action.

In the quiet hills and bustling streets of Rwanda, the echoes of the genocide still reverberate. Let us listen to the voices of those who endured the unimaginable.

Jacqueline, a survivor, recounts the fateful days when the world around her crumbled. "I remember the fear in my parents' eyes as the whispers of violence reached our village. In a heartbeat, neighbors turned into strangers, and the familiar became the unknown. That's when the journey through darkness began."

Separated from her family, Jacqueline's odyssey was one of survival. Hiding in the shadows, witnessing unspeakable horrors, and navigating a shattered landscape, she emerged from the genocide with scars both seen and unseen. Her story is a testament to the resilience of the human spirit.

Jean, a middle-aged man during the genocide, shares the anguish of betrayal at the hands of those he once called neighbors. "We broke bread together, our children played in the same yards. Yet, when the divisions fueled by tribalism reached our doorstep, the bonds shattered. My neighbor, a friend for decades, turned against us. It was a betrayal that cuts deeper than any machete ever could."

These personal stories highlight the human cost of tribalism, where individuals became pawns in a tragic game of identity politics, tearing apart the fabric of communities.

Tribalism, deeply rooted in Rwandese history, was manipulated to sow seeds of hatred and division. The ethnic distinction between the Hutu and Tutsi, once mere descriptors, became instruments of mass destruction. The consequences were devastating, as neighbor turned against neighbor, and a nation descended into chaos.

Survivors recall the dehumanization that became a precursor to the unspeakable violence. People were stripped of their humanity, reduced to mere labels. The poison of tribalism seeped into the collective conscience, turning a diverse nation into a breeding ground for atrocity.

The consequences of tribalism during the Rwandese genocide were profound, leaving a nation shattered and scarred.

Families, the bedrock of society, were torn apart. Brothers fought against brothers, mothers were torn from their children, and homes became graves. The impact of tribalism reverberated through generations, leaving a legacy of pain that continues to shape Rwanda's collective memory.

Communities, once vibrant and diverse, were reduced to ruins. Schools, churches, and neighborhoods that once echoed with laughter and camaraderie became silent witnesses to unspeakable atrocities. The social fabric, woven over centuries, unraveled in a matter of weeks.

In the aftermath of such profound tragedy, the need for reconciliation and healing becomes paramount. Rwanda's commitment to healing and reconciliation is an inspiring beacon amid the darkness. Efforts such as the Gacaca courts, community-led initiatives, and memorialization projects have played a crucial role in acknowledging the past and fostering a sense of unity.

Some survivors, like Marie, embody the power of forgiveness. "I lost my entire family, but I refuse to let hatred consume my heart. Forgiveness is not for the perpetrator; it's for me. It's the only way I can live without being shackled to the past."

The Rwandese genocide offers not only a stark lesson in the consequences of tribalism but also a powerful call to action for the global community. By understanding the devastating human toll, we can collectively strive to prevent such atrocities from occurring elsewhere.

Chapter 5: Irish Slavery - No Blacks Involved

In the annals of history, certain narratives remain shrouded in the shadows, obscured by the more dominant tales that have captured our collective consciousness. In this chapter, we unravel a lesser-known historical event, one that challenges preconceived notions and invites us to rethink the contours of oppression - Irish slavery.

The story of Irish slavery is a chapter often left out of mainstream historical narratives. In the 17th century, during a tumultuous period marked by colonization, war, and economic upheaval, the Irish found themselves ensnared in a web of exploitation that mirrored the shackles worn by other oppressed groups. As the British Empire sought to establish dominance, the Irish became victims of a system that bore eerie similarities to the chattel slavery imposed upon Africans.

Michael, an Irish laborer from that era, left behind fragments of his experience in letters and diaries. "We toiled under the scorching sun, our backs bent beneath the weight of injustice. We were branded as property, our dreams extinguished, our humanity denied. The world may have forgotten our suffering, but the echoes of oppression reverberate through time."

The narrative of Irish slavery challenges the notion that racism is exclusive to one race or group. The Irish, despite being of European descent, faced a brutal system of exploitation that mirrored the dehumanization suffered by Africans. Their plight stands as a testament to the universality of oppression and the capacity for any community to be subjected to the horrors of forced labor.

The chains that bound the Irish were invisible but just as constricting. Stripped of their autonomy, treated as commodities, and subjected to degrading conditions, they bore the weight of a system built on exploitation and prejudice. This lesser-known chapter in history dismantles the simplistic narrative that racism is a phenomenon confined to specific races or ethnicities.

To comprehend the true tapestry of oppression, we must broaden our understanding of history. Irish slavery serves as a poignant reminder that the mechanisms of exploitation are not limited by race but are rather tools employed by those in power to maintain dominance. By acknowledging this shared history, we can foster empathy and solidarity among diverse communities who have, at different times, borne the weight of systemic injustices.

The story of Irish slavery is not meant to diminish or equate the unique struggles faced by different communities. Instead, it is a call to recognize the interconnectedness of our histories and acknowledge that oppression, in its various forms, transcends the boundaries we artificially construct. By embracing the shared struggles of different communities, we lay the foundation for a collective effort to dismantle the structures of inequality.

As we confront the shadows of Irish slavery, we are compelled to question the narratives that have been selectively presented throughout history. By shining a light on this lesser-known chapter, we challenge ourselves to engage with history in a more nuanced and inclusive way. Acknowledging the oppression faced by the Irish underscores the importance of cultivating a broader understanding of the historical forces that have shaped our world.

In the chapters that follow, we will continue to explore untold stories, challenge established narratives, and uncover the threads that connect diverse communities. Through this journey, we hope to foster a deeper appreciation for the complexities of history and promote a more inclusive understanding of the struggles that have shaped our collective human experience.

Chapter 6: Cultural Exchange - Touching Hair

In the mosaic of my life's experiences, there exists a chapter that radiates the warmth of cultural exchange, an episode that transcends boundaries and fosters a connection beyond the superficial. This chapter unfolds in England, a place where friendships were forged, homes opened, and the textures of hair became a bridge between two seemingly disparate worlds.

It all began in the unassuming chairs of a church in Swindon, England, where our journeys converged. Two couples, childless but with hearts brimming with the potential for kinship, embarked on a shared exploration of faith and community. Our friendship extended beyond the sanctuary, transcending the formalities of Saturday services. We visited each other's homes, sharing meals and stories, and occasionally, our evenings stretched into nights.

One particular thread in the tapestry of our friendship was woven during picnics, gatherings that transcended the mere sharing of food. On these occasions, vegetarian dishes adorned our makeshift tables in the country park, and laughter filled the air. It was amid the rustling leaves and the aroma of shared meals that the contours of our cultural exchange began to take shape.

As our friendship blossomed, an unspoken curiosity emerged—one that sought to understand the nuances of each other's identity. It was during one such picnic, surrounded by the serene English landscape, that our mutual interest surfaced in an unexpected and intimate way.

The desire to feel the textures of each other's hair unfolded naturally, a curiosity untainted by stereotypes or assumptions. In that moment, we transcended the boundaries of our respective backgrounds, and our fingers delicately explored the strands that held within them stories of heritage, history, and personal identity.

Allow me to take you into that moment. As the English breeze blew mine and my wife's hair, my newfound friends, with gentle smiles and genuine interest, after asking for permission first, extended their hands. Their fingers, with a tenderness that mirrored the respect between our cultures, weaved through the curls that spoke of my wife's roots, both literal and metaphorical.

In turn, my own curiosity and that of my wife after also asking for permission guided our fingers through the silky strands of their hair. Each touch was a gesture of understanding, a silent acknowledgment that beneath the differences, we were united by our shared humanity. In those moments, we weren't just touching each other's hair; we were reaching across the cultural chasm, dismantling the barriers that often divide us.

Our experience was a microcosm of the potential that lies in positive interactions, where curiosity replaces prejudice and understanding replaces ignorance. In a world often tainted by racial biases, these small yet significant moments become catalysts for change. The act of touching each other's hair was symbolic—an expression of the genuine desire to learn about and appreciate the diversity that makes our world so beautifully complex.

The beauty of our cultural exchange wasn't confined to that picnic blanket; it echoed through our subsequent interactions. Our friendship, strengthened by the understanding cultivated during those moments, became a testament to the possibility of breaking down racial barriers. It emphasized that positive connections can be the antidote to the poison of prejudice.

Promoting positive interactions is not just an individual responsibility; it's a collective endeavor. The more we engage in open, respectful dialogues and seek to understand the stories that others carry within them, the more we contribute to a world where racial barriers crumble, making space for unity to thrive.

As we reflect on the strands of our intertwined experiences, let this chapter serve as a call to embrace the richness of diversity that surrounds us. Our stories, our cultures, and even the textures of our hair are facets of a collective narrative that becomes infinitely richer when shared.

In the chapters that follow, we will continue to explore the beauty of cultural exchange, where curiosity leads to understanding and positive interactions become the building blocks of a more harmonious world. Together, let us break down racial barriers, one genuine connection at a time.

Chapter 7: Acts of Kindness

In the picturesque landscapes of Romania, a chapter of my life unfolded—a chapter woven with threads of kindness and hospitality that exceeded cultural boundaries. As a widowed black man with two small children, navigating the challenges of life took an unexpected turn as the people of Romania embraced me with a warmth that transcended borders.

In the tapestry of my experiences, Romania emerged as an unexpected sanctuary of compassion. The kindness extended to me, a stranger in a foreign land, went beyond the ordinary bounds of hospitality. In a country where I was the outsider, I found myself on the receiving end of preferential treatment that native Romanians seldom encounter.

The first rays of kindness touched me when I was offered more than just a place to stay. It was a home—a sanctuary where the warmth of human connection surpassed the chill of unfamiliarity. In many instances, individuals, moved by empathy, extended invitations for me and my children. The generosity of these gestures went beyond the ordinary; they were acts of kindness that dismantled barriers and fostered a sense of belonging.

As I traversed the length and breadth of Romania, telling my story and encouraging congregants, I encountered hosts who went above and beyond to ensure my comfort. In some homes, they graciously gave up their own master bedrooms, a symbolic gesture that reflected the openness of their hearts. The significance of such acts was not lost on me—I, a stranger, was welcomed into the inner sanctum of their homes, a privilege seldom extended.

Romania unfolded before me, not just as a backdrop but as a living canvas, thanks to invitations that transcended mere hospitality. I was urged to explore regions that many native Romanians had not ventured into. This invitation to travel was more than a geographical journey; it was an immersion into the heart of a country, guided by those who sought to make me feel a part of their world.

In the warmth of Romanian hospitality, I witnessed acts of thoughtful generosity that left an indelible mark on my heart. Some hosts, who owned clothing shops, presented my children with new garments—a gesture that went beyond material generosity. It was a symbol of acceptance, a way of saying, "You are not just visitors; you are family."

In recounting these experiences, it becomes imperative to emphasize the significance of recognizing and appreciating such gestures. Acts of kindness, especially when they transcend cultural divides, are not mere happenstance; they are intentional expressions of humanity's capacity for empathy and understanding. In a world often marred by divisions, these moments serve as beacons of hope, illuminating the path toward unity.

As we close the chapter on the acts of kindness in Romania, the narrative doesn't end; it merely transforms. The next chapter will unveil more privileges, more instances where the boundaries of hospitality were stretched to include a stranger in their midst. Join me as we delve deeper into a journey marked by compassion, generosity, and the enduring power of human connection.

In the chapters that follow, we will continue to explore the unfolding tapestry of my experiences, where acts of kindness become stepping stones toward a world where acceptance knows no borders, and the generosity of spirit binds us all.

Chapter 8: The Ultimate Black Privilege

In the heart of Romania, the canvas of kindness expanded, reaching new dimensions that challenged preconceived notions of privilege and hospitality. The journey continued, leading me to Comanesti, a village where the generosity of the Romanian people surpassed any notion of ordinary acts of kindness. Here, the concept of ultimate black privilege unfolded in unexpected and heartwarming ways.

Comanesti, nestled in the embrace of Romania's natural beauty, became a canvas upon which a unique chapter of my life was painted. In the midst of this tranquil village, I encountered a group of incredibly kind-hearted Romanians who extended an extraordinary offer—a piece of land to build and settle in their community. The gesture was more than an invitation; it was a symbolic bridge inviting me to become an integral part of their village life.

The offer to build and settle in Comanesti was more than a material gesture. It symbolized a profound acceptance, an acknowledgment that transcended the ordinary hospitality I had experienced. Despite the language barriers and cultural differences, the people of Comanesti embraced me, a stranger, and invited me to call their village home. It was a testament to the extraordinary generosity that knows no bounds.

While the offer in Comanesti held the essence of community inclusion, another chapter unfolded in the vibrant city of Bucharest. Here, amidst the hustle and bustle of urban life, I was presented with another remarkable offer—an apartment in Gara de Nord, rent-free for an entire year. The decision to accept this gesture was not merely a practical one; it was a symbolic acceptance of the Romanian people's unwavering warmth.

Gara de Nord, with its eclectic energy, became my home for a year—a year marked by shared stories, cultural exchanges, and the warmth of human connection. My children and I were not merely residents; we were embraced by the rhythms of Bucharest, our lives interwoven with the stories of those we encountered. It was a living testament to the Romanian spirit—a spirit that extends beyond borders and makes strangers feel like cherished guests.

As my time in Romania unfolded, I began to observe a nuanced and complex reality—the perception of black privilege. In a country where my presence was met with warmth and respect, I learned that some Romanians held a belief that black individuals were, in some instances, treated with preferential treatment. It was a perception that transcended mere hospitality; it was a notion that spoke to the depth of respect and admiration some Romanians harbored for people of color.

A surprising revelation unfolded—a testament to the high regard in which black individuals were held in Romanian society. In areas where black doctors or service providers were present, Romanians willingly queued for longer durations, choosing the black provider over their fellow countrymen. It was a phenomenon that defied the conventional narratives of racial biases, offering a glimpse into a unique form of admiration and respect.

Throughout my travels within Romania, I felt the genuine warmth of the people. The acts of kindness were not based on a sense of obligation but were woven into the fabric of Romanian culture. The country became a testament to the idea that true hospitality transcends superficial differences and embraces the shared humanity that unites us all.

As we draw the curtains on this chapter, a teaser for the next unfolds—a chapter where the privileges bestowed upon my young son in Romania will be explored. It is a narrative of joy, of a young soul elevated by the genuine kindness of other children who, far from segregating, chose to celebrate the beauty of differences. Join me as we delve into a world where innocence triumphs over prejudice, and the bonds formed transcend the boundaries of nationality and race.

In the chapter that follows, we will continue to navigate the extraordinary tapestry of experiences in Romania—a country that became not just a temporary home but a sanctuary of acceptance, generosity, and a testament to the ultimate privilege of being seen and embraced for who we are.

Chapter 9: Overcoming Prejudice - School Experience

In the town of Valea lui Mihai, Romania, my son's journey through the educational landscape became a testament to the transformative power of genuine acceptance and the resilience of the human spirit. This chapter unravels the tapestry of his school experiences, weaving a narrative that transcends linguistic barriers, cultural differences, and the innate prejudice that can sometimes accompany them.

Before settling in Valea lui Mihai, my son's educational journey began in Bucharest, where he attended the Valea Lui Mihai school. The remarkable aspect of this initial phase was the heartwarming effort made by his peers to bridge the language gap. Even before he could articulate his thoughts in Romanian, his fellow students took the initiative to purchase English books, aspiring to communicate with him. In a delightful twist, my son, eager to connect with his new friends, quickly learned Romanian, outpacing their English learning endeavors.

His early experiences were a testament to the power of children to transcend linguistic barriers in their pursuit of friendship. The schoolyard, usually a microcosm of societal dynamics, became a playground of camaraderie. In the midst of diverse languages and cultural backgrounds, the seeds of understanding and acceptance were sown, setting the stage for the broader experiences that awaited my son in Valea lui Mihai.

The challenges my son faced, from the loss of his mother to the constant upheaval of moving from place to place, could have easily overshadowed his school experiences. However, his innate friendliness became a beacon of resilience. Even as life presented its complexities, he approached each day with an open heart, eager to connect and share the joy of childhood with his peers.

The charm of Romanian winters, with their massive snowfall, became the backdrop for a heartwarming chapter in my son's school life. In a display of extraordinary kindness, his classmates, far from viewing him as an outsider, treated him with an honor befitting a little privileged prince. When the snowball fights commenced, my son was exempt from the task of making his own ammunition. Instead, his classmates, as though serving a royal decree, handed him the snowballs they had crafted. It was not merely a playful gesture; it was an act of inclusion that left an indelible mark on his young heart.

The ritual of honor extended beyond the playground. Every morning, as he arrived at school, my son was flanked by his friends, as if saluting a royal dignitary. The camaraderie of childhood took on a symbolic dimension, transcending the ordinary interactions of a schoolyard. In those moments, he wasn't merely a student; he was part of a community that saw beyond differences and embraced the shared journey of growth and learning.

These experiences underscore the pivotal role education plays in fostering understanding and acceptance. In the vibrant halls of learning, where minds are shaped and perspectives broadened, the seeds of empathy are sown. The school becomes a microcosm of the diverse world beyond its walls, offering an invaluable opportunity for children to learn not just from textbooks but from each other's stories.

In the classrooms of Valea lui Mihai, where languages intersected and cultural nuances unfolded, my son's journey became a living example of the transformative potential of education. The curriculum extended beyond textbooks, encompassing lessons of diversity, empathy, and the celebration of differences. As children learned side by side, they discovered that the richness of their shared experiences far surpassed any language barrier or preconceived notions.

As we approach the conclusion of this book, a teaser for the final chapter unfolds—a chapter that will reflect on the profound lessons learned, the bridges built, and the enduring impact of the journey detailed in these pages. Join me as we explore the culmination of this narrative—a journey that transcends individual experiences to unveil universal truths about the human capacity for kindness, acceptance, and the breaking down of barriers.

In the chapters that follow, we will weave together the threads of this narrative into a tapestry of understanding, celebrating the transformative power of human connection and the ultimate privilege of being seen and embraced for who we are.

Chapter 10: Unity - Human Connections

As we draw the final curtains on this journey through the pages of "Black Privilege: Transcending Racism" the tapestry of experiences, stories, and reflections converges into a conclusion—a reflection on the key themes that have woven together the fabric of this narrative.

From the shores of Zimbabwe, where tribalism sought to divide, to the snowy landscapes of Romania, where kindness bridged cultural gaps, each chapter has been a thread in the intricate tapestry of my life. The stories shared within these pages are not isolated incidents but fragments of a larger narrative—a narrative that transcends geographical borders, racial lines, and cultural divides.

The recurrent theme of honoring diversity, embracing differences, and recognizing the humanity that binds us all has been the guiding thread throughout. In the midst of historical reflections, personal anecdotes, and glimpses into the kindness of strangers, the resounding message emerges: the richness of the human experience lies in the celebration of our diversity, not in the divisions that seek to tear us apart.

The overarching goal of this book has been a beacon guiding each word, each story—a call to promote unity and harmony among all races. The title, "Black Privilege," may seem paradoxical at first glance, but it serves as an entry point to challenge preconceived notions, urging readers to explore the nuances of privilege, kindness, and the shared responsibility we bear toward one another.

It is crucial to acknowledge that this narrative does not negate the atrocities and injustices faced by black individuals historically and, in many cases, still today. Rather, it seeks to illuminate the silver linings in the rainbow of races—instances where genuine connections, acts of kindness, and the warmth of human interaction overshadow the shadows of prejudice.

As we part ways, my earnest encouragement is for readers to embark on a personal journey of reflection. This is not a call to cast blame or guilt but an invitation to scrutinize our own biases and perceptions. In the mosaic of our minds, subtle prejudices may lie dormant, and it is only through introspection that we can unveil them, acknowledging the imperfections that make us human.

The mirror of self-reflection can be a powerful tool. What biases do we harbor, consciously or unconsciously? What preconceptions shape our interactions with those who may look, speak, or live differently from us? By confronting these questions, we open the door to personal growth and contribute to the collective effort of dismantling the barriers that perpetuate division.

In the spirit of unity and harmony, let this book serve as a call to action—a call to build bridges where walls have stood, to foster connections where divisions have thrived. Each act of kindness, every moment of understanding, and all instances where we choose unity over discord contribute to the collective tapestry of humanity.

The vision of a world where race, color, and background do not dictate the quality of our interactions is not confined to these pages. It is a vision that extends beyond the written words—a vision that necessitates real-world actions, conversations, and a commitment to challenge the status quo.

As we close this chapter, let it be a prelude to the ever-unfolding narrative of human connection. The stories shared here are not singular; they echo the experiences of countless individuals whose lives intersect in the vast tapestry of humanity. By embracing unity and harmony, we contribute to a legacy of compassion, understanding, and the recognition of our shared humanity.

The journey toward unity and harmony is perpetual. It requires a collective effort, a continuous commitment to seeing the beauty in our diversity, and an unwavering dedication to dismantling the barriers that hinder genuine connection. May this book be a catalyst for conversations, reflections, and actions that propel us toward a future where the privileges of understanding, acceptance, and unity are afforded to all.

As we part ways, let us carry the lessons learned within these pages into the world, becoming ambassadors of empathy, advocates for unity, and champions of a more harmonious existence.

In unity and harmony, the journey continues.

www.ingramcontent.com/pod-product-compliance
Lightning Source LLC
Chambersburg PA
CBHW060855260726
48661CB00008B/3277